Pushkar Camel Fair

Beautiful Camels

We are going

to the camel fair today.

Everyone will take their camels to the fair.

This girl will take
her camel to the fair.

This man will take

his camels to the fair too!

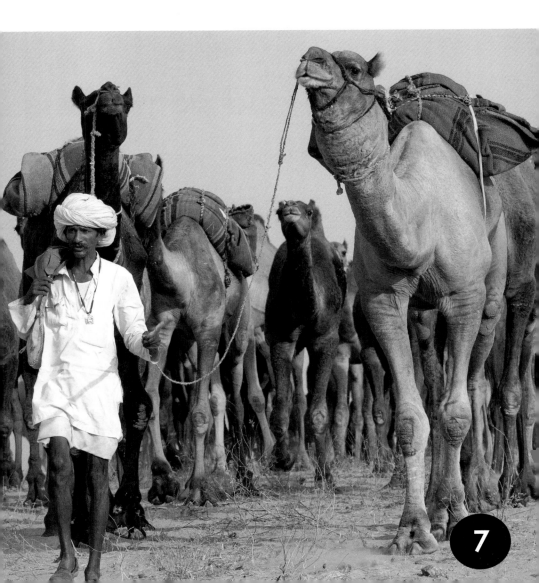

Look at the camel.

It has **beads** and flowers.

It has bells and **pom-poms**.

We will see dancers
at the fair. They will dance
around and around.

Look at the snake.
The man
will take his snake
to the fair.
It will come out
of the basket.

The camel fair is fun!

15

Glossary

beads

pom-poms